Considerations

Poems by Evelyn Klebert

Considerations
By Evelyn Klebert

A Cornerstone Book
Published by Cornerstone Book Publishers

Copyright © 2007 & 2024 by Evelyn Klebert

All rights reserved under International and Pan-American Copyright Conventions. No part of this book may be reproduced in any manner without permission in writing from the copyright holder, except by a reviewer, who may quote brief passages in a review.

First Cornerstone Edition - 2007
Second Cornerstone Edition – 2024

Cornerstone Book Publishers
Hot Springs Village, AR
www.cornerstonepublishers.com

ISBN: 978-1-88756-062-7

Dedication

For My Father,
Billy Webb,
Who Loved Poetry
And My Sons,
Who Help Me See Through New Eyes

Table of Contents

Foundations 1
    A Woman 3
    The House 4
    Hollow Places 5
    She Is 5
    Certain 6
    Ghosts 7
    What About. 8
    New Orleans 9
    My House 10
    Cemetery 11
    Dust 12
Desolation 13
    Vertigo 15
    Tears 15
    Waiting 16
    Past 16
    Lies 17
    The Spiraling Girl 17
    Captivation 18
    Breath 18
    Falling Apart 19
    Falling 19
    Mists 20
Inspiration 21
    Memory 23

Mysteriousness	24
Silence	24
The Edge	25
Questions	25
Rain	26
Strangers	27
Poetry in the Severe	28
A Christmas Poem	29
I Dreamed	30
Considerations	**31**
Essentials	33
I Remember	33
The One	34
Pretty Expectations	34
Holidays	35
Carving out a Christmas	36
Feathering	36
Somewhere in a Quandary	37
Seeds	38
Sifting for Symbolism	39
Picnicking on the Edge	40
Dreams	41
Waiting	41
What is Sown	42
Teachers	43
Forgotten Roads	44
A Space	45

    Moments 46
    Eclipses 47
    Take a Moment 48
    Steps 49
    Life 50
Resolution 51
    Truth 53
    The Light 54
    The Same Place 55
    Seasons 56
    Clarity 57
    A Twisted Road 58

Considerations

Foundations

A Woman

There was an old woman who lived in my house.
I'm more than sure she wasn't always old.
I felt her in the wallpaper,
In the furniture in the spare room.
I smelled the powder she used.
And sensed the heaviness of her sorrow.
She had no voice to tell her pain,
So the walls carried it to my skin.
She wrote me no letters to explain her fears,
So the floors creaked her sorrow-filled tune.
There was an old woman who lives in that house.
I suppose it's still there,
But for her sake, I hope she's not.

Evelyn Klebert

The House

There was a house that should have been by the sea.
It would have been perfect by the water, but it was not.
There was a house where ghosts ran about,
Everyone said so.
But it didn't plague me much.
Maybe they didn't mind me.
There was a house that everyone thought was a problem,
But I thought its curves and bends and unexpected places
Were cozy and unique,
Except that it should have been by the sea.

Hollow Places

I had a doll with a plastic face and eyes made of glass.
Her skin was pale and features delicate.
Her dress was ivory and lace
And I imagined myself as her.
And then I grew up.

She Is

She sits and watches with compassion,
with a need to help in her heart.
She sits and feels helpless,
with only the desire to heal what is raw.
I wonder what she was like younger,
when worry didn't weigh so dearly upon her,
when the world was stretched out before her,
like a rainbow of possibility.

Certain

"I am so certain," she says with a scoff.
The world around me has no clue, she thought.
How bright and brilliant am I
No one knows better than I.
Youth gives a peculiar perception,
A method of rebound that feels forever.
Then years go on, and life continues,
And even the strongest wear down in attrition.
To all of those she dismissed,
She now looks at again, more closely,
And listens contritely.
"I'm not so certain, not now" is the murmur.
And they know, and are patient, because they know.

Foundations

Ghosts

The past is a distant thing,
that doesn't draw breath or reach our world.
It can't scrape its fingers along our reality,
nor tear rips through the thin drape that keeps us
separate.
It can't bring us pain,
nor pierce our emotions.
It can't walk near us
or next to us
or ahead of us.
We can't hear its echoes clearly in a silent moment,
as though those who live there,
are just a footstep away.
It can't do all these things,
be all these things.
How could it?

What About. . .

What about the people you can almost see?
The ones traveling between the flickering of a light,
Who live between the flash of an instant, and
make my infant laugh and giggle with joy.

What about the people who have passed from our lives
But you still feel deep down to your bones
that they wander about,
That they watch you and laugh with you, and
Cry for you when you are lost.

What about the people that you can almost see?
The loved ones that you ache to touch again,
That you need to confide in,
That you need a strong hug from.

What about them.
Are they here right now?
And if I turn around very quickly,
Will I catch that fleeting glimpse?

Foundations

New Orleans

How can you explain it?
It's not something you see,
although it lives in the wood and the bricks,
and the cement.
How can you describe it?
It's not immediately obvious,
though its unique qualities can be described
by those who pass by.
Why is it so special?
Its history radiates from far-off corners,
and its electricity crackles like an old friend
renewing an acquaintance,
one who's been gone for ages,
but now seems only for moments.
How can you explain it?
Why is it different, and why worthy of attention?
You can't.
It simply is.

My House

The house I live in has a sunny shadow.
In the morning the light fills its rooms,
with sweet promises of things that may be.
But as the day progresses and activity continues,
promises are forgotten and living takes hold.
In the evenings when all is quiet,
and the moon casts its luminescence
through an open window,
or just on the shiny cobbled stones in the courtyard,
dreams come to be,
and the spark of mystery takes hold.
It peers through the darkness,
reminding us that we're all
just and only made of magic.

Foundations

Cemetery

Quiet in reverence,
quiet in solitude.
Not a whisper,
not a murmur,
just the breeze whistling.
Some come by,
and the past is stirred,
but then they leave,
and silence resumes.
No one stays here,
it just marks what had been.
The living move on,
and the others had left long before.

Dust

Flies that scrape through the dust,
buzz and dive with irritation,
scrambling along forgotten ledges,
windowpanes darkened from age.
The glass is thinned,
and even the slightest pressure
splinters it into fractures of madness.
When did we become so delicate, so fragile, so weak?
That memories encase us like disintegrating wraps
on mummies in some forgotten tomb.
When did the visions become so fixed
that any breath of life,
sends them cascading into a tumult
into that realm where unreal things reside?

Desolation

Vertigo

I lit my candles,
I drew my bath.
I cleared my mind,
And asked for guidance.
But the pain shadowed me,
And I failed utterly.
So I clung to my ledge,
Drying the tears and hoping
And praying for deliverance.

Tears

They make my face ache,
As they fill up near my eyes.
I work hard to hold them back,
But they're persistent.

Waiting

I suppose it's a mistake to wait.
Waiting for things to come round,
For fortunes to change.
Waiting for dreams to come true,
For promises to be kept.
Waiting for a world I can live in,
Imagining it's just round the bend.
I suppose it's a mistake to wait,
That moment never quite arrives.

Past

I don't like my past,
And dislike spending time there.
The people seem harsher and the emotions biting.
I don't like the light there,
It's dim and uncertain.
I don't like the laughter,
It's hollow and pain filled.
I don't like the past,
And when I see myself there.
I like that least of all.

Lies

Whose lies matter?
Mine or yours?
I told you lies but meant no harm.
You told me lies to keep me near.
My mind was plagued,
Your heart was cool.
Whose lies matter?
Does any of it matter at all?

The Spiraling Girl

I watch her from afar,
Spinning and dancing in a frenzy.
I watch her from up close,
Careening so close to a precipice.
I call to her to wait,
I pray for her to stop.
I've fallen off that cliff before.
You can climb back.
But the price is high and never forgotten.
I watch her spiraling away.
Knowing one day she'll wish she hadn't.

Captivation

What is compelling?
A tantalizing dream,
An exotic landscape
And hopes that unweave.
What insights inspiration,
Desperation of purpose.
The drive to conquer,
The colors of weakness.
What beguiles the heart?
The reality we insist upon
The truths we ignore,
And shred in impatience?

Breath

I'm out of breath,
It fled right out of me.
Surrounded by swirls of panic,
And phantoms attacking.
I'm out of breath,
It's fled.

Falling Apart

I can stand my own hysteria.
I can beat my hands on the floor,
but the thing that tears at me more than anything,
is the sting of your despair,
the tear of your wounds,
the franticness in your voice.
It tears and tears,
so much worse than any wound I can bear.

Falling

Staring down a long tunnel,
endlessly spiraling onward.
From here the words are nonsensical,
then empty,
without texture,
without nuance,
without inflection.
The journey becomes repetitive,
the sensations numb.
The meaning lost,
the purpose intangible.
How did we get here?
How did I?
From where we started?

Mists

I sit on the edge of the mists,
the place just before the fog is too thick to see your way.
I quietly watch you wander from my sight.
I think that perhaps you'll return one day unscathed,
and perhaps you will not.
But it is beyond me now to stop your travels,
and it is quite clear that now I should not.
I myself have seen the pain,
have tasted the dangers,
have bled from the wounds,
but none of it is of consequence.
What drives, drives you fiercely,
and won't begin to cease until it is quelled
from within.
I sit on the edge
and watch you drift away from my sight,
cast further and further away from safe shores.
Perhaps you'll return someday.
Perhaps you will not.

Inspiration

Inspiration

Memory

Walking through halls and forgotten spaces,
wearing the garb of another time,
feeling the emotions that surface from nowhere,
triggered by a word, a gesture, or a thought.
The past is not open for perusal,
but a complicated house,
filled with doors and hidden nooks.
Just when I feel I can finally see it clearly,
another door unlocks, allowing the light
to illuminate its secrets,
to unshroud its truth,
to remember what was lost.

Mysteriousness

The air changes, just a bit,
charges on with an electricness.
The leaves begin to die, but in their demise transform.
The colors inspire but can't be recreated.
Tapped out of strength, tapped out of imagination,
The wonder is elusive and as this chapter closes,
I feel much older, much changed, different in perception.
Different in contemplation as though I've walked,
sometimes run through the longest tunnel, and now
having reached its end
see the world through a new angle.
Good or bad?
Who knows, just altered.
Will everybody know, all the change in me?
Or will what they see seem the same?

Silence

Who would have thought
that I could yearn for such a thing?
I would have never imagined
that this is what I would seek.
The bliss of quiet, not just from without,
but quiet of the mind,
that would elude me.

Inspiration

The Edge

When do you reach the edge,
When your mind says no more can I take?
Is it a decision, or a need to stop the pain?
Is the edge the end, or your decision for the end?
Then sometimes the mind can step somewhere else,
And look inside the chaos from another place.
And the mind can hold itself beyond any pain,
And say quietly.
I am here and can go on forever.

Questions

I can't quite put it together,
Where and why and how.
Where I'm going,
Why I'm here,
And how I can be?

Rain

Watching the rain come down,
not calmly, not serenely,
sometimes in torrents,
sometimes incessantly persistent,
watching the rain come down,
all around me, in everyone's eyes,
watching the rain come down.
And then it stops,
for a while.

Inspiration

Strangers

I see you as a child, so dependent and needy.
Your hands reaching out for my constant care.
A little older, and you're the explorer,
Ravenous to discover,
But my hands still hover,
To keep you from harm.
As your mind absorbs and
Your body grows,
A separate person develops,
That walks further from me.
I give you my stories,
I lend you my lessons,
I work hard to equip you with all you will need.
Then the day grows closer
When your own life will draw you.
And your own spirit will guide you to
An unsuspected fate.
You were never truly mine,
but a fellow traveler like me,
a passerby in my life
that I came to love,
whose presence in my life
was a gift that is unmatched.

Poetry in the Severe

What muffled thoughts roam within my head,
They wander around bumping into odd pieces
of broken furniture,
Furniture that is dusty
Perhaps a little warped, and most definitely well past its time of utility.

The thoughts they wrap around bends and turns,
And fight so desperately to be heard amidst the roar of frantic crowds,
Personages from the past still yelling at me, demanding my attention now and again,
And to make sure that they can still inflict their daggers.

But then there might be a lull for a moment,
The time when I forget to remember,
When sweet peace teases me with the possibility
That indeed what has passed can be released.

It is for those moments that I am still here,
That in spite of the wretched avalanche that invariably follows expectation,
I am here.
And in the quiet, and in the calm, I am set free.

Inspiration

A Christmas Poem

It's quiet through the old house,
although the wood seems to speak itself,
with creaks and noises and afoot when all else is still.
The lights flicker in mutating, colored shapes
across a darkened ceiling,
the only illumination in the room.
And all is in anticipation,
children sleeping
but lightly enough so as to awaken quickly.
Their nerves filled with the awareness
that magic is all around them,
magic whether it be true or be imagined
is real just the same.
An innocent time,
where possibility stretches an endless length.
It's quiet through the old house,
But all is wildly alive in anticipation.

I Dreamed

I dreamed of a love that filled my life,
That inspired and spiraled me into realms of spirit.
I dreamed of a man whose strength enthralled me,
And whose razored mind captured mine.
I dreamed of a man who'd give everything for me,
Who treasured nothing higher than our love.
I dreamed of one whose eyes were lit with fire
From within.
I dreamed of you and thank God for you
Every moment.

Considerations

Essentials

The nights are quiet,
and empty.
Not hollow, as though there is a cavern,
but noiseless as though things are sleeping, hibernating.
It is calm,
a respite from jagged emotion.
Days filled with mechanical activities, externals.
But there is waiting, quiet waiting, expectant waiting.
That any passing, approaching instant the waves will
crash against the shore.
And wildness will ensue.

I Remember

I remember walking through the trees,
but the images are cut soft, not sharp and clear.
I remember voices from long ago,
but the sound is distant and phantom-like now,
not hard and alive, and filled with texture.
I remember what I used to feel,
but I can only remember it now, not feel it.
Was that me in memory?
Or just a fading photograph that time is dulling.

The One

I remember waiting for the one,
the one that made everything make sense.
I imagined what he'd be like,
and then re-imagined him.
I doubted he was real,
then convinced myself he wasn't.
I tried to make others into him,
then gave up, despondent.
I imagined a world without that special one,
and courageously, then cowardly plunged on, into its iciness.
And when I'd finally talked myself into his absence,
I turned around and found him.
Not as I imagined, not as I expected.
But everything I needed and had always wanted.

Pretty Expectations

The pretty expectations line up all in a row,
with whispers and promises of joy
that seem as real as anything that could happen.
Then when they unwind, and unravel before your eyes,
they are mourned with astonishment
as though something that was never real
somehow had been.

Holidays

The holidays greet us with unreasonable hopes of joy.
What normally keeps us satisfied
seems deficient at this time.
The holidays greet us with portraits of life
out of a Christmas card.
We find ourselves dissatisfied,
because what is normally enough is judged wanting.
The holidays bring so much joy to some,
but to others it brings a knife,
cutting, and painful,
where sorrow becomes magnified
in the face of such grand illusion.

Carving out a Christmas

How do people carve out a Christmas,
when life is filled with loneliness and grief
in the moment?
How do people carve out a Christmas when funds are
tight, and it only serves as a reminder of this?
How do people carve out a Christmas when they can
never quite do enough to fulfill their own expectations
or those of those around them?
How do people carve out a Christmas when life feels as
though it is falling apart?
Perhaps with a sigh and a wish and a prayer,
and hope,
Hope that peace can reside anywhere, in any heart,
true hope that peace can reside everywhere.

Feathering

A feathering of ideas swirl in confusion overhead,
waiting for a place to light,
waiting for a place to land, to take root.
An insubstantial prism of possibilities wanders about,
in that quiet, solemn vortex.
And I hope against hope that something will take root.

Considerations

Somewhere in a Quandary

Some steps are bold and definite and easy to understand.
Others are hesitant and trifling and altogether trembling.
Some thoughts are crisp and clear, easily marked.
Others drift and vacillate,
without direction in their intent.
Some days are waiting days,
waiting for a signpost.
Other days are those galloped into action.
The hardest are the waiting ones,
the hardest is knowing soon the waiting
will be a memory.

Seeds

Sometimes the seeds we sow,
seem as though they haven't taken root.
They're so quiet, and so forgotten,
that it seems quite likely they're gone
like a fleeting thought, that simply disappears.
But does a thought disappear?
Or an angry word, or a slanderous comment
to a curious ear.
Does it really disappear?
Or does it just wait, and coil,
and spring to life many seasons later,
only to find its mark,
to do its damage
when least expected.

Considerations

Sifting for Symbolism

Twirling inconsistencies.
Layers deep in shadows.
Hidden places, hollow walls, wails or echoes from unheeded cries.
She swirls down a winding staircase,
her red dress draped,
brushing along the clammy castle walls.
The sunlight greets her,
withering the facade,
burning deeply past deceptions.

Picnicking on the Edge

And before me was the edge of a cliff whose sheer drop
would plunge one to an agonizing death,
and behind me were wild beasts that hungered to tear
their prey into pieces.
And there was no chance of escape,
and only moments before some fatal outcome.
But the moment stretched broad and wide and deep,
and overhead the sky was glistening blue.
The moment stretched into eternity,
and I sat down,
breathing deeply the sweet air.
I perched upon my precipice,
and savored the moment.

Dreams

Shields and wraps of light in dreams
Spots of darkness beyond the seams.
Hallowed prayers and desperate cries
meshing as the sleeper lies.
Swimming toward the surface of the murky lake,
trying to glean a moment for all our sakes.
Wondering what the morning will bring,
beyond the nightmarish landscape scene.
A breath is taken, a sigh escapes,
A whisper of hope, then we awake.

Waiting

The water is at an ebb just now.
Swirling, flowing, churning just out of reach.
I sit on the beach watching, waiting calmly
knowing sooner or later
it will return.
And completely remake the shoreline,
Remolding everything into something quite different.

What is Sown

Turning around, slowly, succinctly.
Knowing that forever changes by the day.
Watching what seems solid shift and then tumble.
Remade into unbelievable, unimagined moments.
Trying to build a future sounds like a shaky prospect.
Thinking that what we expect
would ever truly come to pass.
Instead watching as the seeds flower in surprising,
unusual ways.
And the question becomes whether to embrace or regret
what has only been
in imagination.

Considerations

Teachers

Eyes that are wide but too wise for their years.
Where is such knowledge born?
Lessons learned from children,
who shouldn't glean what they do,
who shouldn't grasp what they can.
Eyes that are wide and are unapologetically blue,
like an ageless ocean whose depths are unexplored.
How can they say the things that they do?
How can they know the truth and accept it so easily?
Eyes that are wide and capture every whisper.
How can they be so young and yet be teachers to all?

Forgotten Roads

Today I took a wild winding road,
down the corridors of a forgotten life.
Shadows had fallen upon the memory,
burying it deeply beneath the fabrics of necessity.
But today, for one brief moment,
it was unearthed.
And I could see clearly where I had traveled from,
the path that brought me to where I stood,
all of it I could remember clearly,
embrace and celebrate.

Considerations

A Space

There is a space,
a pause between sounds.
Not exactly silence,
for silence takes time,
and here time is not involved.
There is a space, a pause between sounds,
when life seems to swirl around,
not quite touching anything.
There is a space,
where everyone is circumspect.
A place of questioning,
and sometimes answers,
a pause between sounds,
that sometimes stretches forever.

Moments

Moments, silent moments become a friend.
Then thoughts sweep in filling my emotion
Good then maybe not
They carve up the serenity with clutter,
shaking my conviction,
questioning, oh just everything.
And then they part, if only for a second.
Reminding me where I should stand and how I had
drifted from it.
Moments I fill with noise,
then silence.
Moments that test me.

Eclipses

We were walking in the snow,
then sledding down a hill.
I stood outside and was overcome by the silence,
then the remote peace that touched the air.
The sun turned red,
and emotions cracked through the quiet,
tranquility dissolved.
Then we spent our time,
in another's history,
in an old house.
It felt like another time,
but then quaked into disarray.
We rippled with events,
thrown about by a merciless fate.
In the midst of a storm, we came home,
and walked beneath a yellow sun.
But memories wrapped around us like serpents
with an unyielding grip.
Spring is coming,
and we walk in its bright new air.
Hoping that grace may yet find us,
and lend us its peace.

Take a Moment

Stuck in a moment,
that doesn't want to budge.
Just beyond it, life turns,
takes a new direction.
Just behind it the past seethes,
and coils and seems to cling.
Stuck in a moment,
that won't seem to pass.
It screams at me,
then whispers kindly.
Look around, breathe in what is here,
for soon it will be no more.
Stuck in a moment,
soaking up what it offers.

Considerations

Steps

If steps are true,
that mark a life,
we travel steep ones
in the night.
Happily, we bound the shallow ones
on bright days,
then hesitate with tricky footing,
when time wears them,
to a splintered or broken ascent.
Perhaps we struggle against the changes,
expecting a path we've envisioned.
Expecting smoothness when there is adversity.
How we greet it,
how we continue seems
the heart of the journey.
How we adjust and continue
seems indeed the key.

Life

There's a texture to life,
its curves and strange arcs.
It eludes predictability,
and often steps outside the conceivable.
It stretches our endurance,
and tears apart our philosophy,
until what was solid,
becomes fluid.
It remolds our ideas,
and breaks apart our beliefs.
It teaches us daily and often,
lest we forget.
That we are the students,
humbled and re-educated
in reverence and wonder.

Resolution

Resolution

Truth

Truth is the crystal
whose light is refracted.
Some see one shard of it,
while others see another.
Pieces of it swirl past us,
and sometimes we catch a glimpse.
And sometimes,
we are simply dazzled by its variations.

The Light

Where is the answer?
We ask in our confusion.
What angle can we view from,
to quell all our fears?
We grasp with intellect,
and lash out with emotion.
Seeking a blanket of reason
to ward away the chaos in which we are covered.
What could we have done?
What should we have done?
What right move could have corrected
What has gone so wrong?
The questions keep flowing
As we swim through our own darkness
we grasp for some light, some help from pain,
the light we can be to one another.
We are each other's healer,
and the hand that lifts us higher.

Resolution

The Same Place

I walked a twisting road
that seems to bend back on itself.
I found myself returning to the same place,
time and time again.
Each cycle I asked, "why do I return?"
but the more progress I made,
the more I ended up in the same place.
So I sat on the earth,
questioning, pondering, then making a new choice.
Not in a rush to leave,
but in a great rush to understand.

Seasons

Before there was the quiet,
where silence took domain.
Thoughts would flow like water,
with mobility — easily, swiftly.
Then activity, sometimes chaos took hold,
and anxiety blotted out the soft murmurs
of a rested mind.
Images came rampant, but jagged and cutting.
Then on its heels the whirlwind,
where change reworked the map.
The change was merciless, yet merciful.
And in its aftermath,
what will be?

Resolution

Clarity

It doesn't arrive in a flash,
in a splendor with fireworks all about.
It creeps in slowly, gradually,
subtly.
It catches you unaware,
but piece by piece everything you thought you knew,
everything you built your house upon,
has been replaced with something new.
It's only when you step back,
and the sunlight hits it quite right,
that you can see it, all of it
put together.
Put together all of it while you were looking off
somewhere else.

A Twisted Road

I traveled down a twisted road.
Its path unclear, direction clouded.
I scraped my feet and tore my clothes.
My skin was chaffed, and raw from cuts and wounds.
And when I emerged, I seemed less to some.
But to others stronger and solid in my determination.
I traveled down a twisted path.
But that journey will stay with me forever.

More Books by Evelyn Klebert

The Lady in the Blue Dress
6 x 9 Softcover & Hardcover 214 pages
ISBN 978-1-61342-600-5
ISBN (Hardcover) 978-1-61342-418-6

When she was a child, Mika Devalieur was introduced to her grandmother's most precious possession — a priceless and mysterious painting that she simply called The Lady in the Blue Dress. Upon Adele St. Clair's death, the painting is left in the care of her granddaughter with only one stipulation. Mika must hand over the family heirloom to a total stranger. Mika Devalieur desperately wants to deny her beloved grandmother's last request, but she can't. Torn between her Gran's last wishes and her desire to hold onto the Lady, she ultimately journeys to rural Virginia, where an enigmatic man shows her that this painting is only the beginning.

What quickly becomes clear is that James Clairmont knows much more about her and the Lady than he is letting on. He begins to slowly unravel a powerful supernatural connection that spans three generations of her family. Mika finds herself desperate to uncover the entire truth before she falls in love with a man filled with so many secrets — secrets about him, about her, and most especially about The Lady in the Blue Dress. (First published on Kindle Vella, episodes 1-23.)

More Books by Evelyn Klebert

Dumaine Street
6 x 9 Softcover & Hardcover 306 pages
ISBN 978-1-61342-902-0
ISBN (Hardcover) 978-1-61342-416-2

Voices in her head, catastrophic emotions, hallucinations – Rebecca Wells is more than convinced that she is losing her mind. And as a last-ditch effort, she contacts a self-professed counselor who seems convinced he can help.

Gabriel Sutton has abandoned the world of medicine to navigate a realm filled with psychic phenomena. Diagnosing Becca with extreme empathic abilities, he struggles to help her stabilize her gifts while trying desperately not to fall in love with his patient.

From the realm of vulnerability into a crusade to use their profound gifts to rescue others from peril on the other side of death, these two follow an astonishing and unpredictable path into each other's hearts.

The Tethering
A Portent of Crows
6 x 9 Softcover & Hardcover 201 pages
ISBN 978-1-61342-599-2
ISBN (Hardcover) 978-1-61342-419-3

Deborah Brandt's beloved Aunt Gena always told her that she was special, a bit different, and would have to live her life, unlike other people. Of course, this she disregarded as the ramblings of her lovely but notably eccentric aunt. Although there were the things that Aunt Gena said that seemed true — like Deborah being sensitive to energy shifts, having potentially psychic impressions, and dreaming of a spirit guide — none of it could be real. But the most ridiculous thing that her Aunt Gena told her before she died was that someone special was out there for her. She said that he was an extraordinary man who was not only her perfect match but someone who she would learn from so that they could help the world in difficult times. How ridiculous! It sounds like a fairy tale, and no such person exists.

Daniel Wren is unique. He has been raised and trained from a young age to hone his psychic gifts. He lives in a world unimagined by most. And he has been waiting for years to contact his counterpart, soulmate, if you will. But the problem is that she is painfully unaware of the type of life that he lives and the life she would be entering into if they came together.

His dilemma becomes how best to proceed. How can he win her over and move forward before outside forces take that decision away from him?

Travels into the Breach
Accounts of a Reluctant Mystic
6 x 9 Softcover & Hardcover 171 pages
ISBN 978-1-61342-323-3
ISBN (Hardcover) 978-1-61342-417-9

At first glance, his life seems quiet, serene, and even uneventful. Malachi McKellan, a 65-year-old widower and author of esoteric books, lives largely as a recluse in a house situated just off the banks of Bayou St. John in New Orleans. But unbeknownst to most, he is also a bit of a detective, a specific kind of detective whose specialty is psychic attacks. Alongside his lifelong companion and spirit guide Simon Tull, a 19th-century, 20-something English gent, Malachi battles the unseen, and is an unacknowledged hero to the most vulnerable. Most of the population have no idea what is really happening beneath the surface of the world in which they live.

In this collection of adventures, Malachi McKellan and Simon Tull wage war against the most insidious elements of the paranormal. In *The Three*, Malachi and Simon come to the aid of a young woman being victimized by a group of dark witches. An old apartment building is the scene of an unimaginable battle against monstrous forces in *The Lost Soul*. Malachi and Simon find themselves strategizing against a psychic vampire in *Obsession*, and *The Hotel* turns back time to the 1980s where Malachi confronts a demonic spirit. In *Between*, a past life is revisited as Malachi attempts to rescue a beloved sister from committing her existence to vengeance, and *The Wedding* takes a personal turn when Malachi must confront painful truths while endeavoring to protect his niece from a potentially devastating union.

Travel into the breach with a pair of paranormal warriors who choose to confront overwhelming forces on a battlefield unsuspected by most.

Gravier's Bookshop
A New Orleans Paranormal Mystery (#1)
6 x 9 Softcover & Hardcover 172 pages
ISBN 978-1-61342-288-5
ISBN (Hardcover) 978-1-61342-411-7

Max Gravier had no intention of becoming a recluse, but after his wife's death it seems his life is heading in that direction. He spends his time running Gravier's Bookshop on Magazine Street and occasionally on the quiet helps the police solve a crime with his psychic sensitivities. That is until he answers Caroline Breslin's call, a cry for help out of his dreams that draws him into a fierce battle for a young woman's soul.

In this first installment of The New Orleans Paranormal Mystery series, Caroline Breslin, an amazingly gifted empath, is determined to strike out on her own and has moved out from the protection of her family home. All is going extremely well until, of course, she comes under siege from a devastating supernatural attack. The last thing Caroline wants is to run back to her family for help, even though she is painfully in over her head. What she really needs is a knight in shining armor — or maybe just that guy that keeps haunting her dreams.

Join them and the whole Breslin family psychic clan in this first installment of The New Orleans Paranormal Mystery Series where you'll travel into a new world just a few steps into the turbulent realm of the unseen.

The Hotel Mandolin
A New Orleans Paranormal Mystery (#2)
6 x 9 Softcover & Hardcover 146 pages
ISBN 978-1-61342-290-8
ISBN (Hardcover) 978-1-61342-412-4

Peril is wrapped up in the most enticing of disguises in *The Hotel Mandolin*, the second installment of The New Orleans Paranormal Mystery series. It's opulent, classic, and one of the most renowned hotels nestled deep in New Orleans' famous business district, but something is amiss at The Hotel Mandolin.

PI Peter Norfleet is calling out the big guns to help him investigate a recent suicide at the famous establishment — his good friend Max Gravier, a formidable psychic, and his girlfriend, Caroline Breslin, a talented empath. But none of them can seem to scratch the surface of this puzzle, no one except Cassie Breslin, Caroline's clairvoyant mother, who has somehow tapped into an unexpected connection with a tragic ghost from the turn of the century. And the more she uncovers, the more dangerous and malevolent the mystery becomes

The House at Pritchard Place
A New Orleans Paranormal Mystery (#3)
6 x 9 Softcover & Hardcover 138 pages
ISBN 978-1-61342-292-2
ISBN (Hardcover) 978-1-61342-413-1

Nothing is really wrong with the old Warrick House on Dante St. except that there most certainly is. Nothing is exactly wrong with its new mysterious owner except that Elise is sure that something doesn't add up. It isn't obvious, but sometimes the most dangerous things aren't.

In the third installment of The New Orleans Paranormal Mystery series, with the help of her very psychic sister and her children, the Breslin clan, Elise Ashford is about to embark on a wild rescue mission straight into another dimension that will land her squarely somewhere she doesn't expect, right back into her past. She'll land full circle; in a childhood home whose memory still haunts her to this day -- *The House at Pritchard Place.*

More Books by Evelyn Klebert

Treading on Borrowed Time
6 x 9 Softcover & Hardcover 223 pages
ISBN 978-1-61342-214-4
ISBN (Hardcover) 978-1-61342-436-0

For Julia Moreau, life seems complicated. Emerging from a failed marriage and managing a lifetime of diabetes, she lives alone in her childhood home where she communicates with the spirit of her Great Aunt Lilia. But Julia doesn't have a clue what complicated is until she is thrust into being the key chess piece in a match between two powerful men of extraordinary abilities on the wild hunt for a mystical creature hidden in the heart of New Orleans' French Quarter. Will Julia lose her soul to the karma of a devastating past life or her heart to the love of a man driven by dark forces? What is clear is that whichever way she turns she is *Treading on Borrowed Time*.

Sanctuary of Echoes
6 x 9 Softcover & Hardcover 371 pages
ISBN 978-1-61342-211-3
ISBN (Hardcover) 978-1-61342-409-4

Ghosts unacknowledged do not sleep.

Corey Knight has resigned herself to a quiet, reclusive life spent living out the rest of her days in her childhood home on the fringes of New Orleans' French Quarter. But the unexpected specter of her deceased father plunges her into a mad quest for a missing supernatural weapon unearthed long ago. And unfortunately, her only ally is a lost love she once betrayed.

Iain Shaw returns to New Orleans, a city he abandoned a decade before while fleeing a devastating past. Here, he is forced to confront it again in the visage of the woman he once adored - one that he is now determined to get back at any cost.

Follow them both in a wild paranormal tale of discovery and redemption as they confront and unearth the echoes of a buried and unyielding truth that once tore them irreparably apart.

A Quiet Moment
6 x 9 Softcover & Hardcover 273 pages
ISBN 978-1-61342-326-4
ISBN (Hardcover) 978-1-61342-435-3

Jacob Wyss is caught in a rut, in fact on the verge of being engulfed by it. After an excruciating and disillusioning divorce, his life as an artist in a sleepy-college town at the foot of the Appalachian Mountains has become quiet, routine, and maddening in its predictability. One wintry day, his deep restlessness drives him out in precarious conditions to a largely empty bookstore nearly devoid of another living soul, nearly.

Aimee Marston isn't like everyone else. On the surface, she lives a sedate life working as a feature writer for a small local newspaper in addition to several other editorial jobs to help make ends meet. But just beneath, her existence is largely not her own. She is a sensitive, an empathetic psychic, guided by her calling to use her gifts to help others. Unfortunately, as a result, her secretiveness has made her defensive, protective of herself, and prevented her from having much of a life.

A psychic call for help sends Aimee out on a freezing January morning where her destiny and Jacob's collide sending both their lives spiraling onto an unexpected and often disturbing track. Two lonely souls connect, not by accident, but by design. Theirs is the intersection of two spiritual paths, two lovers who must struggle to overcome the phantoms of a past life, as well as the challenges of their own inner demons to carve out an extraordinary future together.

A Ghost of a Chance
6 x 9 Softcover & Hardcover 230 pages
ISBN 978-1-61342-162-8
ISBN (Hardcover) 978-1-61342-440-7

You never know what's coming next.

Jack Brennan, an ambitious high-powered attorney, dies. But that's not the end, rather only the beginning. He finds himself constrained to an inexplicable afterlife as an earth-bound spirit trapped in an old Virginia farmhouse. His only companion is a very much living, reclusive writer of campy vampire novels. The maddening problem is that Hallie does not know he is there, nor that he is somewhat reluctantly falling in love with her.

Hallie Barkly is recovering from a painful and disillusioning divorce. Out of the ashes of her former life, she has managed to somehow forge a career and exorcise her demons by writing under the pseudonym of Sebastian Winters. Slowly, she is awakening to the fact that she is not alone.

Their lives intersect, and two unconventional lovers are brought together under insurmountable circumstances. Together they must battle an unseen force hell-bent on possessing Hallie's life and bridge death itself to make possible what cannot be — to find a chance.

More Books by Evelyn Klebert

Dragonflies - Journeys into the Paranormal
6 x 9 Softcover & Hardcover 176 pages
ISBN 978-1-88756-072-6
ISBN (Hardcover) 979-8-32548-418-6

In every form of creation, there is a blueprint for living, for experience, for interpretation. In flight, they can twist, turn, alter direction, pause in midair, and even fly backward. The dragonfly is the master of adaptability. They are a living prism, refracting light, and color, seemingly shifting their essence.

The lesson the dragonfly gives is that life is never what it appears to be.

In "The Wizard," as a novice practitioner of magic, Aurora Finn finds herself battling against the illusions of a powerful wizard intent on separating her from the world she knows. "The Sojourners" is a gentle story of a mother and daughter whose tenancy in an old Virginia farmhouse uncovers the trials and sorrows of its former occupants. A bookstore clerk gets an extraordinary customer on Halloween night in "Late One Night at Berstrums Books." In "The Tear," a woman coping with her fatal illness unknowingly begins a track on a mystical journey that will entirely restructure her vision of the world.

These stories follow the path of the dragonfly imbued with the momentum and energy of change, taking a winding and treacherous journey that ultimately leads to truth buried beneath perception.

More Books by Evelyn Klebert

Breaking Through the Pale
6 x 9 Softcover 134 pages
ISBN 978-1-88756-045-0

Journey with metaphysical author Evelyn Klebert into a collection of short stories that travel beyond the pale into the unpredictable realm of the paranormal.

In "A Grey Mourning," a disillusioned man encounters a mysterious being on the foggy streets of New Orleans. "Contact" is a tale of automatic writing, when a young artist establishes communication with a spirit guide, and the victim of a car crash unravels the true nature of her existence in "Dancing on the Threshold." The final tale is called "Isolation," in which a confused and disoriented woman finds herself in an old, quaint house where she must piece together the mystical implications surrounding her predicament.

Explanations
6 x 9 Softcover 82 pages
ISBN 978-1-93493-515-6

In this, her second poetry collection, Evelyn Klebert takes us down the intricate path of a personal journey. Life with its particular struggles, pitfalls, and ultimately triumphs clearly begins to mirror a universal path, the quest for answers that we all ultimately pursue. In this reflective, esoteric collection we can all explore and seek some of life's elemental mysteries and hopefully when all is said and done emerge with some *Explanations*.

More Books by Evelyn Klebert

The Witches' Own
6 x 9 Softcover & Hardcover 140 pages
ISBN 978-1-61342-058-4
ISBN (Hardcover) 978-1-61342-428-5

On the surface things seem quiet and serene in the picturesque coastal village of Kilmarnock, Virginia. But something unseen roams its lush forests as the past and present collide and the unthinkable begins to wreak its vengeance. Young Lucy Bonner is executed for witchcraft in the town's distant and brutal past. Her death triggers an unholy chain of events which grasp at the restless heart of novelist Peter McQuade, spurring him towards a quest to uncover the dark and terrifying truth.

The Left Palm
And Other Halloween Tales of the Supernatural
6 x 9 Softcover & Hardcover 122 pages
ISBN 978-1-93493-556-9
ISBN (Hardcover) 978-1-61342-442-1

Halloween is the time of year when that veil between worlds is thinned, and you can just catch a quick glimpse into the realm of the unknowable. In this collection of short stories, Evelyn Klebert takes you to a place where ordinary life splinters into the sphere of the paranormal.

The journey begins with one woman's unstoppable quest for vengeance against a supernatural creature in "Wolves" and continues in an old historical graveyard where a horrifying discovery is uncovered in "Emma Fallon." In "The Soul Shredder," a psychiatrist's unusual patient opens his eyes to a disturbing new view of reality, while in "Wildflowers," a woman strikes up a supernatural friendship with impossible implications. And in "The Left Palm," a fortuneteller in the French Quarter receives a most unexpected and terrifying customer.

White Harbor Road
And Other Tales of Paranormal Romance
6 x 9 Softcover & Hardcover 152 pages
ISBN 978-1-61342-066-9
ISBN (Hardcover) 978-1-61342-441-4

A psychic soul mate, a time traveler, a horror writer, and an enigmatic stranger take a selection of resilient, life-battered heroines to a place of paranormal healing and transformation. In this collection of short stories, *White Harbor Road* is the last stop where life's burdens and hardships evolve into something unexpected.

The Broken Vow
Vol. I of The Clandestine Exploits of a Werewolf
6 x 9 Softcover & Hardcover 204 pages
ISBN 978-1-61342-133-8
ISBN (Hardcover) 978-1-61342-420-9

In the heart of every man there is a history. In the heart of every monster there is a story. In this first installment of *The Clandestine Exploits of a Werewolf*, Ethan Garraint is on a vendetta that begins in the heart of the Pyrenees with the fall of Montségur and leads him to the streets of New Orleans nearly five hundred years later. But the person he chases isn't really a man anymore and Ethan has been a werewolf for almost a millennium. With the aid of a gifted seer, he is on a blood

More Books by Evelyn Klebert

hunt that will culminate in a journey that crosses the line between heaven and earth and ends somewhere in between.

Appointment with the Unknown
The Hotel Stories
6 x 9 Softcover & Hardcover 155 pages
ISBN 978-1-61342-360-8
ISBN (Hardcover) 978-1-61342-421-6

A hotel, for most, represents a normal place, a predictable realm of commonality. One might even go as far to say a safe space, the reliable where nothing particularly unusual is expected to happen. Or is it? Dimensional traveling, spirit guides, mystical storms, and soul mates separated by time are only a few elements dotting this supernatural landscape. Drop into a collection of romantic paranormal stories where that place of commonality is only the threshold, the jumping-off point, for extraordinary adventures into the unknown.

Visit Evelyn's website at:
www.evelynklebert.com

Cornerstone Book Publishers
www.cornerstonepublishers.com

www.ingramcontent.com/pod-product-compliance
Lightning Source LLC
LaVergne TN
LVHW041345080426
835512LV00006B/612